BURNING
PROVINCE

BOOKS BY MICHAEL PRIOR

POETRY
Model Disciple

BURNING PROVINCE

POEMS

MICHAEL PRIOR

McCLELLAND & STEWART

Library and Archives Canada Cataloguing in Publication

Title: Burning province / Michael Prior.
Names: Prior, Michael, 1990- author.
Description: Poems.
Identifiers: Canadiana (print) 20190162317 | Canadiana (ebook) 2019016235X |
    ISBN 9780771072345 (softcover) | ISBN 9780771072352 (EPUB)
Classification: LCC PS8631.R575 B87 2020 | DDC C811/.6—dc23

Published simultaneously in the United States of America by McClelland & Stewart, a division of Penguin Random House Canada Limited, a Penguin Random House Company

Library of Congress Control Number is available upon request

ISBN: 978-0-7710-7234-5
ebook ISBN: 978-0-7710-7235-2

Typeset in Birka by M&S, Toronto
Book design: Leah Springate
Cover image: © CSA Images / Getty Images
Printed and bound in Canada

McClelland & Stewart,
a division of Penguin Random House Canada Limited,
a Penguin Random House Company
www.penguinrandomhouse.ca

1 2 3 4 5   24 23 22 21 20

Penguin
Random House
McCLELLAND & STEWART

For my grandparents and my parents

CONTENTS

BURNING
PROVINCE

A HUNDRED AND FIFTY POUNDS

> *Each adult will be allowed 150 pounds*
> *and each child will be allowed 75 pounds of baggage.*
> —B.C. SECURITY COMMISSION, 1942

after Kayla Isomura's The Suitcase Project

In some, the luggage lies open
like a mouth mid-sentence.
In others, closed zippers grimace:

What would you have brought?
Slippers, a stuffed platypus, a gold watch
on a chain, copper pots swaddled in bedding.

The hypotheses: that thinking
can be things, that each decision shrinks
the pained mind to the space

inside a suitcase. Include
lacquered chopsticks, silver forks,
a hammer scarred by rust, the orders

nailed to telephone poles and doors.
Omit what you whispered then,
most of what you've seen.

I was given forty-eight hours' notice, twenty-four.
I passed ice and pines and plains.
I rode an iron serpent

into the Interior
beside four hundred others.
It was humid. It was cold.

If pain is remembered
to be dismissed. If fear still seeds
its rotting forest. This

is a gardener's trowel, a blue skein of yarn,
a violin, a ukulele, a ukulele, a ukulele.
This is a porch light

flicked on and off in abscessed night.
These are pear blossoms falling
on the driveway like footprints in black ice.

Memories, river stones,
metamorphic and worn. How many
might an able-bodied individual carry

through livestock-stalls and mud,
onto a bus, a train,
into a tiny, uninsulated shack?

Most say the same: *It could happen again.*
It is happening now. I couldn't
make room

for a dogless collar,
a hound's-tooth scarf, a steel urn
packed in Styrofoam, a letter

recording blood's divisive fractions.
My father would not have come.
My mother. My stepsister. My brother.

What matters is not what you bring,
but what you keep.
She was there. He was, too.

SELF-PORTRAIT AS A PORTRAIT OF MY GRANDFATHER, DECEMBER 8, 1941

If a memory bears radiation's
relationship to time; if his eyes are
and are not mine; if strawberries once
rotted in muddy crates on a farm
unfarmed and seized. Then, a reborn face's
parabolic features curve an axis
never crossed; then, salt and silver nitrate
scribe light's dictation on the page

of them and us—of me and him—of fear's vindictive
aperture and frame. Of how what's outside
fades what's within—or how a cold sun gathers in my eyes,
my hair, my mind, like half-lives
borne on wind. How half alive and half asleep,
each waxen pore's single seed.

AUCTION

A house with a broken face
facing the strait, an eviction pinned and fluttering
against the door. A trawler's
dry rot above the sea, and higher, a bristling wreath
of gulls. Their hollow marrow,
their ampersand hearts. You passed from here
as photograph. You passed
as a current through storm-downed cables, intractable
signals curdling water, air—
in a lifetime, this will all be bound by water, the geologist said
atop the crumbling peninsula
while looking a little too pleased. Burnt vines frayed
the trail. Blackbirds hemmed
thorn and shadow. Whose lifetime anyway? His? Yours?
We weary improvisers
scabbing our hands in the bracken, shifting frames
along the mantel—our aim,
no more than the careful arrangement of dust. How
carefully you would unstitch
the thorns from my skin. Now, sallow headlights crawl
across the kitchen glass at night,
as if in search of water. The sink fills itself with sand.
I wanted to be the one
to tell you this—to miss you best. When the land is gone,
meet me where it was.

THESEUS'S SHIP

Summers, they drove us to Steveston.
Even then, he didn't have a single one
of his original teeth. Seagulls and terns

massed above the seiners bloodying
the Pacific. Each season, new boats
worn older—old boats painted new. Once,

from the corner of my eye, I saw a red bird
plummet through the waves—or was it a white bird
reddened by the sun? Salmon, mackerel,

haddock, sole: they quivered in their beds of ice.
Some mornings they drove us to the pool.
We dived through the lukewarm chlorine

after dimes. Her smile: more gold and arsenic
than bone. I hate to say I thought of this
when I unboxed the ashes packed in Styrofoam,

or, worse, that I can't recall which of them
first showed me how to hold my breath, make
my body a star, so I could stay afloat.

LIGHT AND YEARS

I remember how she rewound the VHS
each time I pleaded to see the *Falcon*
sail free from a dead star's fiery pointillism.
Or, how he leaned back, answered, *We waited for it to end*,
when I asked, *What did you do in the camp?*
Years later, it's difficult to say who
first described the midnight funerals,
the way rows of tarpaper shacks roiled
in recollection like sap boiling beneath its grain,
the black hole of a body unbodied by heat.
Neither knew the names of the deceased.
What did they feel, then, watching again and again
while the sky bowed its damp forehead
to the flames—wind unfurling birchbark
in striated swathes of white. For a cheek's
burst capillaries, glaucoma's blizzard in an eye,
conjure older worlds, constellations
burnt out before we see them. Still, we see them.
I couldn't wait to unwrap the blistered
cellophane: a foil-lit galaxy's stippling,
the rock salt that flecked the frozen asphalt
of their South Vancouver home. *Patience,*
patience—then a sidereal scroll of names and places
I couldn't read flashed past their hands,
darkly knotted over the couch cushions—mine
knuckled pallid during that final scene,
where dead fathers, living daughters, and unborn sons
wait by the fire for an obsidian mask
to fill with ash—to unbecome its pain. Difficult
to say we watched it again and again.

and the breeze that salts the air
with a storm's ionic aftertaste. Along
the boardwalk's nautilus, tourists pin themselves to the clouds
on selfie sticks. Beneath, runoff
from the tankers slakes the pier
with sulphur rot. Sulphur
in the river. Sulphur plumbing the bones
of the birds shipped from across the sea. The flowers,
too, were brought here: they survive
in brackish water, secrete
a resin that burns skin—light
darkening a darkroom's silvered paper,
or this print in which my grandfather presses to his mother's
dress in a too-large Sunday suit.
The flock's wings were first
clipped before the War.
Now, flash-floods swallow
shallow nests, and twice a year I return for family, for friends,
for faces dissolved in vistas mostly water—
see both wave and body swell,
then cease. The New Year
curls in the bud of the Old. There is a song
that begins *less lonely less*—another that ends *it doesn't matter*.
What else did he mutter that night we flung
our bottles into the delta's froth?
They glowed like seiners
through the fog. Night merges
the river with the mainland. Cygnets unreel snails from shells,
strip stalks to their wet marrow.
I watch the late-season

blossoms blister and fall:
paper lanterns climb the breakers
in my grandfather's eyes. He regards the lens like a door
shut suddenly by wind. The irises anchor their fronds
among the driftwood. They hold on
as he once held both his mother
and another, severed by the frame.

TASHME

Taylor, Shirras, Mead

At ten, I thought it sounded Japanese—
the name no name but acronym, initials.
Older, visiting in winter, needles
fall from the pines like chaff's steel-
storm across my face.

Is this the signal or its foil?
That I thought the name was Japanese.
The valley channels what's left of a coastal breeze
scattering deadfall's initials
across what snow's erased.

RICHMOND

    after Katherine Anne Porter

Where are my people? Past the cannery
sloughing into ocean and the maples
reddening shallows along the overpass,
you say, *It's all water under the bridge.*
So, I wonder which bridge. Behind: the bonsai
choking on its dollar-store pot, and the cat,
who belongs to no one and therefore
everyone. *The basis of human relations,*
you explain, as our car compasses the bay.
And my own time? When frogs roiled
across the highway slick with rain
and herons swayed on stilts, waiting
for the storm to cease. The shidare we failed
broke its spine's lightning crease. Sludge
dulled the sidewalk, crows coveted
nightfall from the eaves—louder, even,
than the thunder. The mud drained from
my boots like a leash or a line tied to gravity,
tied to sea. *And what horse shall I ride?*
The dark one. The bright one. The one
without eyes. The one thrashing among
the cranberry bog's weave. The one that missed
the sugar in your palm, leaving scars
I mistook for seams. The one that wore
through the steel of his shoes. The one you told
to not look back, who did, and saw you were
afraid. The one who never looked like
a horse. Or the one that stretched its neck
and tore the last leaf, dripping, from the tree.

She said, *Forget the dishes*, and, *He hit me with a wooden spoon*
              until I bled. Passed from one family
to another in the camp, she wore tin cans like stilts, drew circles
              in the dirt. *She wasn't my mother*
at first. Terrible at blackjack, Texas holdem, her stepfather
              sent letters frantic for cash. Each written
in a different hand. Penticton. Kelowna. No Japs from the Rockies to the sea.
              Baskets of Braeburns. Serene, the orchard's
auburn waves of leaves and branches. School all day, worked until
              she slept. Ironed and swept. Fried
kippers and eggs. Put someone else's kids to bed. The smell of dried fish.
              Everyone fights sometimes. It's fine:
they fed me every day. Her husband shouted in his sleep about sawmills,
              houses built from dust. She
tended theirs, pruned the garden's rising swathes of summer.
              There was too much left unsaid.
To me: *Shikata ga nai*, and, *Leave your sister alone*. She liked
              pickled shiso, Sir Roger Moore,
and Hallmark Christmas ornaments. Disliked: flying and talking about
              the past. Once, I watched her feed sugar water
to a honeybee with a spoon. Silver coins she couldn't afford slipped from
              her palm to mine. She said, *Don't tell*
your mother, and, *Farted is an excellent word*. A man lost all her money
              twice. Saltwater. Slatted blinds.
Sallow moon that spawns along the Fraser. Riverside apartments
              in diminishing square-footage.
Coquitlam to Richmond, Richmond to Surrey. That undistinguished
              block of Hastings, where her
stepmother's shop once stood. In front of us, she never said her given name.

PORTRAIT OF MY GRANDMOTHER AS THE BURNING PROVINCE

Where were you amid the water?
Viscous, thickened with bone for a weakening throat,
it arrived in unmarked cartons
while your skin scrolled off and your hair
lay plastered to the bed. *More
please*, you said. Inland, blue pines candled troughs
of soured milkweed, leaves cindered boughs,
pallid mansions in the clouds—

and on the sixteenth floor, men in paper masks
drained radiated litres from the yellow bucket
beneath the bed: *biohazard*,
it said. You, already husk and halving,
watched breakers of ash collapse towards the coast.
Now, when I dream, I dream everything but the smoke.

WAKE

The mirage's voices,
        a burning door.
You, a broken TV's wavering screen:
        I'm waiting—
please come back.
        I woke and was on a train:
everything past the glass
        sweltering, in blossom.
Those younger summers,
        we picked blackberries
beside the burnt hulks
        that lined the tracks.
I woke and was on a plane,
        the clouds lit soft like ash,
while somewhere below, away,
        your hair wiped free in clumps
under the damp pressure
        of a cloth. Asleep,
you clutched your red cardigan:
        cardinal weathering a storm
beneath folded wings.
        I woke and you spoke
in a tongue of smoke—
        of lotus leaves shivering
in a downpour, flocks
        scattering from their roost.
I woke and it hadn't rained
        for a hundred days;
the slatted blinds
        combed clotted light,

the ward as warm and curdled
        as your breath.
Outdoors, smokers sought
        shade's receding wave.
I reached for a berry set in thorns
        and split my thumb,
a thermometer's single vein.
        On the red-eye back,
I had slept until the tarmac's
        asphalt sea. Late, afraid,
I waited in the hall
        before knocking on the door.

In cloud country, water has but two states:
we feel the crease between a wave and its cold,
between us and the sun. In cloud country, your mind
settles its mist across the TV's broken screen,
the IV's taped labels, the metal rungs strung
along the bedframe, like ladders into a hidden room.
Here, Kyushu is a doorway left ajar, a nightlight's
shadow shift. Here, we admit ourselves
the paper's ninth and impossible fold—the way
we say, *Hello*, meaning, *Hold on a little longer.*
Or, *I don't know*, meaning, *It's true.* Errant cells spill
like sea salt over the corridor's mirrored linoleum,
as we shuffle from floor to floor, and you live
long enough to see your glasses return to style,
your plaid shirts, your knit cardigans. Within our borders,
your hair frays cirrus into sky, while that bride,
so serious in every photo, never had to be you. Drowsy,
draining through a plastic tube, in cloud country,
you say, *That was all so long ago*: each closet
a mossy gate, each wormwood cabinet a cabin
dissolving in your nowhere backwoods,
where the plural is story, the singular skin, and the notice
stapled to the door does not make of one face
many. Was there ever a quiet street, a pink bungalow,
a trio of hunched maples, a cup of cooling sencha
waiting in this nation for you? In cloud country,
you say, *It feels like I'm being eaten*, and choke down
spoonfuls of ice-cream, lemon jello. We thicken
your water with powdered bone. In cloud country,
the horizon doesn't sever the sky, but spills upwards,

a helix of white smoke, burnt leaves. While the fledglings
in our chests bear no desire to leave the nest,
or rot to barbed wire. At this latitude,
the textbooks declare the heart an un-cracked
robin's egg—the mind, a clever mockingbird's—
and every morning is the morning
you showed us the bitterns, curtained by bulrushes,
towering in their sleep. You closed our eyes
as we passed the one broken on the boulevard.
It is here that you promise to reveal
how to uncrimp each beak from its paper bud,
how to unfurl each wing with the perfect pressure
of fingers not yet talons, veins not yet tunnels
of wind and sleet. It is here that you mutter, *I had a name*
so that we understand: every animal has wings.
No dignity in indignity, you kept it all to yourself
in cloud country, where the sheets folded you
and the crinkled gown exposed you; where the swallows
never stood still—and never stood
for want. We kept them to ourselves. We kept this
for you. You plead, *Leave a window open,*
a skylight unlocked. We flatten our faces
against the glass's double-pane. We couldn't
finish those final folds alone. You left us
for an image of astounding order. There was
no order. We listen to the radio for your whereabouts
until we, too, bear throats wracked by static,
blistered with Coriolis. The fields that stretch
behind the boulevard rise and evaporate easy
from their bedrock—now, no different than bed.
In cloud country, it rains newspaper cranes, it cries
Fujita scale, it hears your tectonic mumble merge

with ours: there is no scale for now and then.
You are the paper's one hundred and third fold,
the nebula's gauzed edge. In cloud country,
you say, *Thank you.* We say, *Thank you.*

WHETHER

To speak of the *ever*?
The *never after*? Water begging of dry weather

a place. Looking back,
which was less than have and more than lack?

To recall our pity,
recall the fireflies, building their burning city.

PROVINCE

When you wake to ash on the cars
and warnings strung along the causeway,
leaves lying winded in pools.

When smoke scales the towers crowning the bay,
and a crane's metal scaffolding
seems a hammer

held to fall. Or when you watch
the shimmering meniscus recall
where you dipped a single, calloused toe. This:

when echo crosses echo;
when of them, only the heavier sound still tolls.
As when you marvel

at the nimbus's dissipation under sun
or when the corgi you walk strains against the leash,
believing she's close to home.

And when home approaches evening.
And when evening sieves the birches' zebra skin
from the lake's ripe, hurried swells—

why leave or linger?
For when once there was rain's
dark and downward kingdom,

now, only a slowing susurration
and the bees that pour forth from the dead cow's hide
like embers from the wettest flame.

For when drought carves from every forest
its bones, or when each word
consumes the one before, watch

the cardinal
gathering dry grass and bracken
flare at his reflection in the pane.

GRANDFATHERS' AXES

Have I told you the one about the chickens?
Ash-handled, flecked with rust
each leans behind its box of kindling,
inside different cabins on different lakes. One
belonged to a grandfather who wore ugly sweaters,
sold rivets and rebar up and down the coast.
The other, to the other—whose brother
left him a folio of hand-drawn instructions
for folding paper cranes. If a tree falls in a forest.
If a man falls on a basement treadmill,
or on an ice rink's refrigerated plane—
who's the first to answer the ringing phone?
One listened to the goalie recount how he held
his skate-blade against the lips to check for breath.
Another lay inert, while his daughter
locked her fingers and hammered along his ribcage
as if trying to find a hinge. *Have I told you
the one about the chickens?* They were
stupid kids. They were stupid drunk. Once,
after the War, they stole a couple roosters
from a neighbour, and with his brother's hatchet,
cut their heads off on the beach. Once,
after haying, he and his son stole the rancher's hens
and hid them in the woodshed. The sand was red.
The shed was white with floating down.
It was dinner. It was a joke. In the drawings,
there is one that with the proper folds, will flap its wings
when you pinch the centre of its breast. One kept
trying to speak. One only blinked. I pick out
the splinters, having no callouses on my hands.

II

STEVESTON

Night clots across
the pockmarked snow. A pug grunts,
then crumples in a doorway's furnace-glow.
It scours its paws with salt and looks
toward the docks. Born into the taut orbit
of a leash, does it know

it wouldn't float? When young,
I believed in hard work's volition. I no longer
feel the same—only the same worm scrivening
the heart. As a sharper monk once urged,
*In all things, the beginning and end
are most engaging.* Which is which

depends on who speaks for whom, and when,
and why I can't decide between
what's theirs and mine, our differences'
stark differentials of time and comprehension
like the names that braid each other's spines,
the blackberry's escarpment

of barbed wire— *Steveston, Sutebusuton.*
Gold reminds my finger to another.
Foxtails rustle radio silence over
the delta's muddy skein. Rain follows snow:
a hangover's erosion of a dream.
At least it's easier to shovel. For now,

it's too dark to see the water,
but I hear its groan and patter
against every surface that won't give. All around
frost scales the million-dollar homes
that box the mausoleumed shipyards,
the cannery's museum

where placards evaluate degrees
of heritage, of *here it was*.
This tires me: to make of each wave
the sea. An asphalt lot spans civic
and community centres.
Above a gilded eye tracks movement

beyond the keen—
wings gargoyle then melt
into the fraying trees.
When my mother asked,
How does it feel to be back?
I heard myself say, *The same.*

PASTORAL

Wildroses, horsetails, wind's cobwebs over water:
summers here since I first learned to swim.
The poplars across the bay shimmer and sway,
reflections creasing under the weather
like molten glass. To think that *mirror* once meant
both *to wonder* and *look back*—the way
I've stared into a funhouse pane and seen my mixed face
split then doubled.
                   North, the rocks are choked with millwort.
South, starlings rustle through the cedars:
brought by a man who spent his life importing
every bird in Shakespeare. New worlds
forever measured by the Old. For every measure,
an equal and opposite erasure. How, over the fire,
the family friend said, *Jap*, not Japanese.

VOLE

The vole clock, you said, *is how we date unknown strata.*
The vole clock, you said, *is their teeth*:
each bicuspid plucked from dirt, a stone seed,
similar and strange as a vowel's unfamiliar intonation

in another time and place: how five centuries ago
love rhymed with *prove* and *prove* with *drove*,
as in, *We drove along the highway built by my great-*
grandfather during the Internment, where once

grey foxes churned like runoff behind the chicken-wire
of their cage—raised and sold for rations,
fur matted, they pressed their snouts to the mud
and dreamt of burrows deep as vowels,

far from them as language. When they cried,
they were birds fallen from the nest.
Have you seen that documentary—an arctic fox
stalking across a sea-change of snow and cirrus? It lunges

through the white, then surfaces,
a tail dangling from its jaw like a second tongue.
I walk past rabbit-brush, scrub birch, willow,
branches bare of Cameo and Empire. To mistake an order

for our own: this orchard's symmetrical plots
of graft and growth, its gardens recreated, re-arranged
by era and nation—their purpose
anachronistic to their presence. The fence's winter foil

keeps us in and out. Beside the herbarium's copper marker,
my mother rubs dead hemlock
between her hands as if testing it for threadcount—
Don't worry, I'll just Purell—

around the corner, my father, supine on ice
proffers birdfeed to a shadow
that darts between his palm and the dark,
filling its cheeks with seeds. How could something

that looks like fear be fearless? Which one of us said,
Just leave it alone? Time casts itself in cold.
Of the voles, you told me, *They huddle together:*
they have been proven to comfort each other

in moments of duress. Our duress,
momentarily our own. Of that documentary,
my favourite part is when the fox dives
and you can hear the narrator's escaping breath.

Wind stirs the roadside dogwoods into static. Framed
        by the windshield, a pair of swans nose trash along a ditch;

wings open and clench in argent fists. I sit passenger-side
        to my father, while border guards parse our

where and from. The space between as vast as the river
        that renews its boundaries beneath the overpass, before

the waterfall's pulsing cobalt. How old was I
        when his mother wished my brown eyes would fade

to blue? Along the window, late-season cabbage moths
        skirt updrafts through the dogwoods, wings blinking

against the guardrail. Aluminum barns dot the borders
        between home and stead. Waved through, I nod,

eyes down. *Of course he's my son.* The highway: riven
        with meltwater. Time: calving, ice-clad, inexorable

as Occam's razor. Later, park benches fur with frost
        and I sit beside my mother watching a storm's wet pressure

vein the lake. Nearer, two gulls trace figure eights. *So where are you from?*
        the man at the gas station asked. For the sum

to displace its ratio, read: *What are you supposed to be?*
        The place between, as overcast as the cold-

front overhead. Once, her tired father declared his nation hyphen
at the border—wrote *Canadian*, then, before it,

Japanese. He was detained. Muddy snow piles along the treeline
like a picket fence in need of paint.

MINORU

The horse in my mind
is not the horse in the park,
his canter bronzed beneath maples
and a plaque blazoned *Minoru*—

Minoru, says my mother,
de-emphasizing the expected syllable
as if the word were Japanese. Home for winter:
pines and cedars merge in the car's convergence
of distance and speed. They bow to each other's shadows. I want

to run further
than I can see.

Minoru, churning clods
of earth as he rounds the track
at Doncaster. Minoru,
Thoroughbred, bred

to step lightly,
lightly stepping
through snow's patina
along the steppes, where he rests,
time cindering his name.

But before the horse,
the master gardener from Kyushu,

whose green thumbs
grew sore with expatriation,

razoring lawns across the cold hills
of Kildare, twisting hedgerows

into mazes, pruning moss as soft
as a stallion's foam-flecked mane.
For his talent: a horse to share his,
youngest son's name. Minoru. *Of course it's*
Japanese. Of them, who was furthest from home: father, mother,

mixed-race son?
The park and the track

flicker into frame, our breath
fogging the windshield's washed-out
glass, faces folding time—that portrait
in which the gardener holds his eldest like a dove,

while Minoru sits alone
on his mother's lap. *Why the long face?*
my mother asks. She drives the speed limit,
comes to a complete stop before every line. We pass
the track, the statue, mane ribbed mid-sway as if subject to the same

wind shivering
the branches.

Minoru, victorious, mimetic
in oils for *Vanity Fair*, painted
by Earl, by Havell. His glossy wake, a wave rippling
top hats and swallowtail coats, dark as storm-bruised water.

Minoru, thundering into the final heat at Epsom.
Minoru, snorting under King George's gouty hand.
Minoru, of the Triple Crown, the Irish downs, swallowed up
by a crowd of supporters pulling hairs from his mane and tail.
For hair's curlicue on canvas: feel the pressure of the brush.

Crop to stirrup. Bridle
to spur. Once,

I watched my mother
mourn her mother. She
used a name I can't pronounce—
issei, nisei, Okaasan—liquid lilt

of a seashell's hum, voices
hushed behind closed doors.
Though raised mostly in English,
in college she was forced into a beginners' class.
She waited. She passed. When we pass the statue, she laughs.

Mom, how could the name be Japanese?
Statue, park, and ruddy track remade

from recycled tires,
where for years in elementary
I ran the hundred-metre dash
while she applauded from the stands. Only

ever silver, never
quick enough. As a girl,
she rode the neighbour's worn-out hot-blood

after school. No saddle, just a wool blanket folded in half.
He would gallop the same counter-clockwise loop along his paddock's

muddy acre, habit's burnished track.
She gripped his mane and never fell.

You know, I can't remember
what he was called. Their lives dissolve
in mediums as amnesiac as water: Minoru's father
returned to his island to die. The horse, foundered,

and nearly blind, was sold across the ocean
into a revolution's measure—a motion
spent like crests collapsing against the coast.
In the kanji that she can barely read, one shoulder is turned

as if to recall receding miles. *Uma*, meaning horse, or, *I'm sorry, Ma.*
Her maiden name:
a copse of trees.

They shiver when I turn
the page. From ten thousand feet,
the ochre track is a serpent
circling the unknown at the edges

of a Renaissance map. I wave,
and again I am alone. The window's scratched
acrylic, a dead stallion's eye. Each sentence I try
is built from words like the wood in Theseus's ship. The boy, now
lost to a century's blueblack ebb like snow into the sea—

Don't be such a precious snowflake,
my mother says.

The stallion: one win short
of the Triple Crown. My intonation:
one stress too many for an apology,
all the times I got it wrong. *Minoru,*

Minoru—both are gone.
Their twinned weight sinking back
through the past like the rings
passed hand to hand in the chapel beside the park,
the track, the statue, where years ago

my mother said the word
and took my father's name.

MY FATHER'S BIRTHDAY IS THE DAY BEFORE MINE

The last train pulses across the pane
and fireflies spark beside the tracks.
Acne's red wing flames my face:
I can't take back

this skin. In the other room,
a drugstore Timex synchronizes
with the faucet's drip. If I squint,
the fireflies align their lives

to map the summer's migraine
of flowers that were weeds.
You say, *but I think*
they're just trying to survive—

cheap bulbs, they burn out in two weeks.
The train rattles as its links shift
and scrape like the dark between days.
From across the continent,

my father texts:
your mother hiked halfway up the hill
behind the cabin /a graceful
mountain goat. Is this love?

Lately, I've been writing you letters
that I shred about that blood-orange eclipse—
sleep's determined murmurs
of eyelid and lash.

The fireflies are sunset's ash.
I realize I have no means
by which to make you a present of the past,
where my father once cowered

behind the June sunflowers,
bloodied by the dog-chain his father
had swung—not at his son,
but at the fear

of being left without one.
The fireflies stutter like an apology.
I would be lying to you
if I didn't admit I love them.

WHITE NOISE MACHINE

He can't sleep without the sound, and I can't sleep
because of it. Driftwood itching seashore, sleet
muffling a skylight's December dark.

This: not art but element. He can't sleep apart
from it. It's the wind that winds the birches'
phantom limbs, their arteries of sky. Who can hear

for all our static? The highway hums across the glass.
We flicker past a pair of swans nosing trash
along a ditch. The windshield's tint of blue, the hue he seeks.

Blue: the reason he can't sleep.
I sit with my father beside the lake, as the lake
renews its boundaries. We watch a pair of gulls trace

figure eights. He can't wait for sleep without
its pitch, without it sieving air. A decibel oscillates
his mind, then mine. He can't sleep
without the sound. I can't sleep because of it.

POEM AFTER THE GIFT OF AN AMMONITE

for Ammons

I saw my imagined nation nest in yours.
Flurries spiralled across the windshield:
pines bent their backs into the wind. Here,
where nothing new falls or grows,
where the weather bruises into kin,
and where each approaching car
glows a backlit aquarium, I wondered what it meant—

this gift. Like a careful florist,
snow stripped the fences of their barbs,
smoothed the buried faces that dreamed this plain
a plain. To think that given an inch,
you graved a mile's grey imagination: that light
atop the tower striating into a line of distant others
when I shifted lanes. How to say

we're all from elsewhere,
really? How to say, somewhere, past Elmira,
I glimpsed the Pacific in matter's merger
between states: slush broke against a John Deere's
beached hull—home frayed across a blizzard's dull teeth.
It took a while, but the feeling passed
as you, or what was left
of you among the windbreaks

thin as widow's peaks: a breath's brief plume
of ice and air. Had we met,
I think we would have gotten along—
would have driven out on days like this

to listen to the highway's unspooling cassette,
its hum curling in our ears like the dead sea
frozen in that fossil, your name

asleep in a stone
whose spiral segments hoard their centuries
as a pane of glass hoards molten sand;
or how, once, in a landlocked town,
I looked through a library's well-lit window
at the night that had swelled when my back was turned
and, though I tried, saw nothing else.

NEW YEAR

I've resolved last year's resolutions
watching this bonfire fail to flame.
I've ignored December's iterations,
unsolved my consolations:
a card, a call, a paper crane's blame-
less fractions of the same.
I can't solve for time's absolutions
watching these embers fail to flame.

SALAMANDER

Rain boils the river.
It sloughs its silver into the canals that cut
the city blocks. Tonight, her hands emerge

from behind amber glass intact,
then submerge and shatter. On my way here,
couples bloomed in unison

along the Commons: they huddled under
umbrellas—slick and glistening,
dark as a Victorian garden. I'm listening

to her voice falling in my ear,
the roof's faint patter when she texted,
if it wasn't so late, we could look for

salamanders. My mind circles, stirs
its bowl of smoke. Later, she will admit she wants her,
and I'll admit this syllogism's

shadow creature. The candle on our table
twitches, twists, lets slip its flame. Her fingers
cup its spectre, muscles gripped

amphibian in skin. *What I'm trying to say*
may not be what I mean. The lack
of light swells, scatters,

exhaust crawls toward our chins.
I know where they live. Where the puddles
flood and merge; where the road bisects

the woodland; where we'll soon part
for our homes—the searchbar's scroll
of strangers and estranged, frame and picture:

I saw one of a limb lost and regrown
without pain. I saw another of a species
starred with fire. They sleep in the Niagara basin

and breathe through their skin. It doesn't matter
that they are born without ears.
They still hear the falling water.

NEVER BEEN BETTER

We put too much trust in Google Maps,
but arrived regardless. The guardrails
girding the boulevard: distended
under ice. The slate shined a snail's
hemoglobin stain. There was no rain.
Where the ambulance

and the funeral home share an owner,
it's best to only be passing
through. Amphetamine squirrels
thrummed shadow oaks. Cats stretched
into stillness as if to sun.
My best reflection remained

a revolving door's tinted glass
as we exited, older, onto an unpaved street.
You: a design that described time
while being of it. By the end,
I was so moved I couldn't move.
This wasn't the intent—starlings

massing a single mind above
the slatted fields, the suburban creep,
the tentworm constellations. Everyplace
three, three and a half hours away.
We blew a tire on a pothole
outside Penticton, past countless flags

limp on sills, and a wrong way sign
hung upside down. In town,
kids sloshed along the riverbed
with buckets and nets. One was saying,
I'm sorry. Another was cupping
something in his hands.

CAMPANOLOGY

I'm tired of sleep—tired
of belief exceeding its cause,
of love curling in the telephone,
subtracting week from month and month from year,
bodies striating bedsheets like waves of sound.
Are you there? I couldn't tell
you about the time I saw the deer, how their delicate faces

seemed nearly human, or how,
wavering in likeness,
they beaded free, one by one,
from pools of lamplight.
I heard nothing as they passed. It was night.
Now, morning breaks like a vase
dropped from the hill, where the clock-

tower hammers the nascent hour:
crystal-faced and faceted, it seems an insufficient vessel
for its sound. In the park,
the green is freshly cropped.
The wind snags on my rougher features.
Here, a solar system fixed in concrete
shadows light-years along the canal

while mallards ripple emerald
in the eelgrass: some tempt the storm-surge
then vanish through the dark
that lingers, still, under the bridge.
I miss your call. The bells begin

the hour again. Some days, they play
"Don't Stop Believing." Some days,

"I've Had the Time of My Life." But most often:
"Happy Birthday." Happy birthday.
We both are twenty-six. Twenty-six
in total, composed of a particular alloy of bronze and tin,
the bells speak only of and through collision.
I squint into the wind and watch the grass bend,
the water glisten, listening.

THE NIGHT

Morning in the city we watched the rays
kite counter-clockwise loops
along the aquarium's
plaster simulacrum.
Stingers clipped,
they brushed our fingers
with their smiles. In another room rank with ozone,
the eel roiled in its globe,
bound to human boredom
by glass and steel.
Twin poles rose
from the turbid murk
to chain its current
while a string of lights flickered each time it smeared
its snout against
the pane. Porcine, garish,
nearly eyeless: the nightmare
or the night. We
muscled to the front
while it cut figure
eights through the mud, as if searching for its missing
limbs. I couldn't help
but think of the ink
winding up your arm,
the clockwork scribed
across your spine
by some ex–Hell's Angel
on the island—how that first time in a room lit
through rain, I saw another us
move beneath our skin.

There, where I pressed
my lips, proof for Balzac's
dream of the self
as a million memories
burnt into a nerve—so nervous, I almost couldn't.
All this: mnemonic
for ink, for implication,
for Balzac, whose heart
burst five months
after he first wore
the ring. Your hand
wandered the tank's patina of past fingers.
I wondered but didn't
ask your thoughts.
We left, and behind us
flowed the human crush.
Down the corridor,
your grip curled mine
in kindness. The lights flicked on and off.

TASHME

There's a wedding today.
Groomsmen in rented carapaces
stake signs beside rotten porches
and scintillas of RVs. *This way
to the reception*. We watch as they straggle
into a Jeep, retreat behind tinted panes
past where the shacks once stood.
Everywhere, elsewhere:
the highway's hush hush of wheels
and a breeze that sways sedge and skeleton weed,
dandelions and thistles—soil's
indifferent genius. By the creek,
red-winged crickets flutter and snap
like fans. Wasps rest on sweet peas' trellised lips.
That ancient agrarian insists, *It's time
to lift the harnesses from our horses'
lathered necks*. They're a stretch,
these contiguities between land and mind—
but consider the speed limit:
over a hundred the whole way back
to Hope. There's nothing to see, really.
There's nothing to be seen. North, northeast,
fires metastasize through the Interior,
though we can't glimpse the smoke.
I want to say something callous
about the heat. I want to ask when will it begin.

THE LIGHT FROM CANADA

Falls over the brushed steel
of Ontario and Erie, rises where the floes
fracture and dissolve.

Is it true that the first things we read and feel
never leave our vocative?
A darkling thrush, a darkling plain,

the eye's search for the mind's glinting level.
To say the light *falls* or is *from*
is misdirection:

it has no discernible mass,
belongs to no one.
I worry about you, said my grandfather

for whom my feelings
remained irrevocable. I had thought myself
worried for him, too. It was late:

we ate blackberries from an earthenware bowl,
drank instant coffee, and stood
by a bonfire in the rain

because it was New Year's,
and he had no home
he could return to.

Where I grew up,
vines barb the highway, bridge the ditches,
as if desperate to prove themselves

necessary to a whole. There is a hole
at the centre of every knotted mass,
a nebula of mold.

Some nights I worry
I've studied the field-guides
more than the fields: *Here is blackberry;*

skull-weed; eelgrass; there,
the canker rose—names that rise into place
like the lenses that fell

between my eyes and a wall of wordless letters
while someone unseen
repeated, *Is this clearer, or this?*

GEORGIC

This is the landscape
I was made for,
where the work
is a word half-recalled,
unpronounceable
without practice,
or a story in which
my great-grandfather
tends a strawberry farm
in a small town
beside the Pacific:
the rotting mulch,
the suck of mud on a boot,
vines' frost-stunted fruit;
the way the ocean
nested driftwood
across the frozen beach,
or the time a nest
of field-mice ruined
the only rice for months—
vignettes I had to hear
to see. Today, I eat
strawberries in bed and sleep
until the sun raises
its bright meniscus
over the brownstones,
the endless meiosis
of the off-ramp,
the median's poor

attempts at colour:
early magnolias, narcissuses,
clumps of parched crabgrass.
I have heard, too, how
my great-grandfather
died of tuberculosis
in a northern city,
having left his wife,
his children, the farm,
to travel across the country
to study the lucrative
sculpture of false teeth.
Somewhere, in an Ontario attic,
there is a leather satchel
filled with his tools:
a fine-stemmed mirror
like a flower stripped
of petals in a game
of he-loves-me-not;
a steel drill, its bit as thin
as a hummingbird's beak.
And somewhere,
inscribed on each,
a name I couldn't say
without having heard it
said first. Tomorrow,
when a late snow
gathers along the sidewalk
like bone-light in an x-ray
I will stay inside
and imagine its cold

dissolving on skin,
its wet weight
tugging on a heel.

WAKEFUL THINGS

You should never put the new antlers of a deer to your nose and smell them.
They have little insects that crawl into the nose and devour the brain.
—KENKŌ, *Essays in Idleness*

Consider that the insects might be metaphor.
That the antlers' wet velvet scent
might be Proust's madeleine dipped into a cup of tea
adorned with centrifugal patterns of azalea
and willow—those fleshing the hill behind this room,
walls wreathed in smoke and iron, musk
of the deer head above the mantle. He was nailed in place
before I was me. Through the floorboards,
a caterpillar, stripped from its chrysalis by red ants,
wakes, as if to a house aflame. Silk frays
like silver horns, like thoughts branching from a brain.
After the MRI, my father's chosen father squinted
at the wormholes ravelling the screen
and said, *Be good to one another.* Love,
how inelegantly we leave. How insistent we are to return
in one form or another. I wish all of this and none of it
for us: more sun, more tempest, more
fear and fearlessness—more of that which is tempered, carved,
and worn, creased into overlapping planes. The way
I feel the world's aperture enlarge in each morning's
patchwork blur of light and colour while I fumble
for my glasses beside the bed—lenses smudged
by both our hands. When they were alive,
those antlers held up the sky. Now what do they hold?

"Mute Swans, Yellow Irises" borrows from Robert Hayden through Eduardo C. Corral; the poem is for both of them. "Tashme" was the name of the largest Japanese Canadian internment camp in British Columbia during the Second World War; it was where my grandparents and their families were held. The name is an acronym derived from the surnames of the B.C. Security Commission officials who organized the Internment: Taylor, Shirras, and Mead. "Richmond" riffs on Katherine Anne Porter's story, "Pale Horse, Pale Rider." "In Cloud Country" takes its title from James Merrill. "Steveston" regards a remark from Kenkō's *Essays in Idleness*. "Pastoral" considers an aside in Annie Dillard's *Pilgrim at Tinker Creek* about Eugene Schieffelin. "Poem after the Gift of an Ammonite" is for Alice Fulton. "Province" and the second "Tashme" listen to Virgil's *Georgics* (trans. Janet Lembke); the second "Tashme" also includes a phrase from Robert Lowell, and alludes to the forest fires that in 2015 and 2017 consumed thousands of hectares of the province of British Columbia; in 2017, over sixty thousand people were forced to leave their homes. "Never Been Better" misreads a phrase from Joan Didion and a couple more from Michelle Orange. "The Light from Canada" takes its title from James Schuyler. "Wakeful Things" is for Cody.

ACKNOWLEDGEMENTS

These poems have recently appeared (occasionally as earlier versions) in the following publications. Thank you to the editors.

Academy of American Poets' *Poem-a-Day* series: "Wakeful Things"
Ambit: "Auction" and "Salamander"
Asian American Writers' Workshop's *The Margins*: "Minoru"
Contemporary Verse 2: "Vole"
The Fiddlehead: "Province"
Great River Review: "The Night," "Theseus's Ship," "Wake," and "Whether"
The Literary Review of Canada: "Steveston"
The Manchester Review: "Light and Years" and "Mute Swans, Yellow Irises"
Narrative: "Campanology"
The Next Wave: An Anthology of Twenty-First Century Canadian Poetry:
   "In Cloud Country"
PN Review: "New Year" and "The Light from Canada"
POETRY: "My Father's Birthday Is the Day before Mine"
Poetry Northwest: "Pastoral," "Poem after the Gift of an Ammonite," and
   "Self-Portrait as a Portrait of My Grandfather, December 8, 1941"
The Puritan: "My Pronunciation Was Wrong," "Never Been Better," and
   "Richmond"
The Walrus: "Grandfathers' Axes" and "In Cloud Country"

Thank you to Dionne Brand, Kelly Joseph, and all the great folks at McClelland & Stewart. Thank you to Alice Fulton, Ishion Hutchinson, Jim Johnstone, Catriona Wright, Kayla Czaga, Nyla Matuk, Korey Williams, Vincent Hiscock, Mario Giannone, Cary Marcous, and Ben Voigt for reading earlier drafts of this manuscript. Thank you to Carl Moon, Phoebe Wang, Masha Raskolnikov, Pumpkin Raskonikov, Alexandra Chang, Mary-Margaret Stevens, Christopher Berardino, Aurora Masum-Javed, Helena Maria Viramontes, Stephanie Vaughn, Michael Koch, Cristina Correa,

Annie Goold, Rocio Anica, Neal Giannone, Robert McGill, Richard Greene, Lyrae Van Clief-Stefanon, Gina Machida, my cohort at Cornell, and my colleagues at Macalester College for friendship and feedback. And, of course, thank you to my family, especially Cody.

Necessary funding and support were provided by Cornell University and the Canada Council for the Arts. Thank you to both institutions.

MICHAEL PRIOR is a writer and a teacher. His poems have appeared or are forthcoming in numerous magazines and anthologies across North America and the U.K., including *Poetry*, *The New Republic*, *Narrative*, *Ambit*, *Poetry Northwest*, *The Margins*, *PN Review*, *Verse Daily*, *Global Poetry Anthology 2015*, *The Next Wave: An Anthology of 21st Century Canadian Poetry*, and the Academy of American Poets' *Poem-a-Day* series. He is a past winner of *Magma Poetry*'s Editors' Prize, *The Walrus*'s Poetry Prize, and *Matrix Magazine*'s Lit POP Award for Poetry. His first full-length book of poems, *Model Disciple*, was named one of the best books of the year by the Canadian Broadcasting Corporation. Prior holds graduate degrees from the University of Toronto and Cornell University. He divides his time between Saint Paul, MN, where he teaches at Macalester College, and Vancouver, B.C.